Translations by Alfred Cahn and Miriam Ben-Shemuel
The intent of these translations is to provide an understanding
of the meaning of the lyrics. The translations are not literal
and therefore, will not fit with the music.

Hava Nagila
Let's rejoice,
Let's sing and let's be happy.
Utter a song, brothers, with a happy heart.

Zum Gali Gali

Zum Gali Gali

"Zum Gali Gali" cannot be translated. It is equivalent to a
humming sound and has no other meaning.
The last two lines translate as:
The pioneer is made for work.
The work is made for the pioneer.

Hatikvah

As long as there is, deep in the heart, a
Jewish soul vibrating, our hope is not lost
yet: To be a free people in our land,
the land of Zion and Jerusalem.

Hatikvah

Espressivo ♩ = 69-72
Israeli National Anthem
mp Kol - ohd ba-ley - vav pe - nee - mah Ne - fesh y'-hoo - dee
hoh - mee - yah, Ool'- fah-ah-tey miz - rach kah - dee - mah
Ah - yin le Tzee - yon tsoh - fee - yah. Ohd loh av - dah
tik - vah-tey - nu Ha - tik - vah shnoht ahl-pah - yim,
Lih -yoht ahm chof-shee be - ahr - tsay - noo b'eh - retz Tzee - yon vee - roo - shah-lah - yim.
mf
mp

Purim Day

Traditional
English words by E. Fragen

Mazel Tov

Mazel Tov
Good luck to the groom and bride.
We sing to all, a good holiday today.

Avinu Malkeynu

Hevenu Shalom Aleychem

Avinu Malkeynu
(This is only a small part of a solemn prayer.)
Our Father, our King, be gracious and answer us,
for we have little merit.
Treat us generously and with kindness,
and be our Saviour.

Hevenu Shalom Aleychem
We brought peace upon you.

Artza Alinu

Moderato ♩ = 112-120
Folk Dance
mf Ar - tza___ a - li - nu, ar - tza___ a - li - nu, ar - tza___ a - li -
nu. Ar - tza___ a - li - nu, ar - tza___ a - li - nu,
ar - tza___ a - li - nu. f K' - var___ cha - rash - nu
v' - gam___ za - ra - nu, K' - var___ cha - rash - nu v' - gam___ za - ra - nu,
A - val___ od lo ka - tzar - nu, A - val___ od lo ka - tzar - nu!